STITC

Stitches

KATE SCOTT

PETERLOO POETS

First published in 2003
by Peterloo Poets
The Old Chapel, Sand Lane, Calstock, Cornwall PL18 9QX, U.K.

**A catalogue record for this book is available
from the British Library**

ISBN   1-904324-11-8

Printed in Great Britain by
Antony Rowe Ltd, Chippenham, Wilts.

ACKNOWLEDGEMENTS

Acknowledgements are due to the editors of the following publications in which many of these poems first appeared:

Envoi, Magma, The New Writer, Other Poetry, Oxford Poetry, Poetry Nottingham, The Rialto, Tears in the Fence.

'Reading a Biology Book' was highly commended in the 1996 National Poetry Competition.

For my mother

Contents

Teenagers Waiting at the Station

Fourteen or fifteen years old,
their voices not yet stretched into shape,
they bluster on to the platform.
They have a sulky look, a look still unsexed,
their sallowness waiting to ripen.

They lean, tucked into corners,
their limbs taken from mannequins,
ill-fitting, awkward, crude.

There is something veiled about them,
their eyes lowered or glazed,
like the sly lids of geckos basking on walls.

Up close, they smell of fusty shut-up rooms,
cigarettes sneaked through window cracks,
medicated face wash, fresh sweat.

They dream of being men, of walking in the wide spaces.
Meanwhile, they share their fears without words,
the astonishment at this disconnection, this treachery
as their bodies speed ahead and leave them behind,
like a train suddenly split to two different tracks.

They are steeped in longing,
taut and nervous as colts with the waiting.
They tense with the urge to autograph,
to leave a mark, a stamp, a cry,
to use the voice they know is disappearing daily,
while there is still time.

Warning

I hated sports at school. While I grew,
it was as if the expansion of cells sapped my blood,
making me lumpen and unready as raw dough.

So that afternoon, when the animal pulse perked up
and sang through the veins of The Others,
I turned pale and weak as skimmed milk.

Even my clothes knew of my inadequacies.
The creases fled from my red nylon skirt,
the white shirt bulged out everywhere except my chest.

My glasses were held on by elastic.
My hands flew up to my face
like protecting birds checking their roost.

The teams were picked. I was not first, but not last.
It was, as always, a mean-mouthed triumph.
It was kill or be killed, the last were lost.

We were fielding.
I took myself out to the furthest spot,
ground as yet undiscovered by the swing of bats.

The Others would need to be superhuman to hit like that.
My inner thighs rubbed damp together in prayer
to the God of Miserable Teenage Girls.

No doubt she was busy.
The next moment I heard my name like a gunshot
the ball – a harbinger of evil – following directly after,
for a second even blocking out the sun.

It streamed towards me,
laughing through its seams.

My cupped hands pleaded,
trying to entice its landing
with whispered obscenities and prayer.

The world yelled with the fury of Amazons at war.
The ball swept quickly into my hands . . . then changed its mind,
leapt out. I scrabbled on the ground and threw it far enough to be free.

Disgusted, the world turned away and played on.
I stood shaking, the shame spreading like a hot flush, dying my skin.
And then, trembling with rage, I planned my revenge.

Only the losers are safe.

Ants

When intoxicated, ants always fall to their right.

Imagine the certainty of drunken falling!
To know you will always fall right.
To become adept at a graceful lunge,
to know which arm to tuck like a wing,
to know which space to clear with your slurring feet.

Imagine watching from the top of a trapeze,
the scurry, the scuttle, of insect people.
Your stomach cradling itself in the pit of your belly
but the exhilaration in your chest!
The euphoric, inebriated, united descent, to the right,
to the right, to the right.

Religion

Children are vicious puritans,
spitting out the indefinite like greens.
So in a household with shrines
to liberal sophistication
I followed a religion of blasphemy.

I turned the spare room into a church,
annointing anyone passing
with tap water and solemnity.
Christened at seven, I was happily cloistered
in a high-collared white dress like a miniature bride.

I took myself to church on Sunday evenings.
There were five of us including a young man
with a long coat and slicked-back hair.
He smiled too much and the old ladies smelled
and I didn't like being on my own.

Taken to churches and cathedrals in the name of art
I embarrassed my mother by falling to my knees.
Religious sensibility not running in the family
she worried that people would stare.
Unencouraged, I drifted away from God.

Today, I am uplifted by the sun of an afternoon,
watching objects in and out of rooms
illustrate light.
I think of the eskimos with hundreds of words for snow,
emphasising weight by variety of definition.

I wonder if I passed or failed a test in faith,
thinking of snow which weighs nothing unless pressed
and disappears on examination.

There

There, you say, as you wind sheets round me
and the shivering slows to a tearful judder's rhythm.
There, there, and the word is tender as your fingers to my back.
There, you whisper later, bodies overtaking
voices in forgiveness.
There, I pick my favourite patch of skin, and rest my head,
to investigate your heart.
There, where I thought we were, on the map of us, upside down.
There, where you say we are, newly changed, your hatched emotion
in me already fledged.
There, within a breath I feel we could be, balanced in flight,
and trying to grow new feathers of faith, in us, in you.
I watch you sitting there and wonder, sneaking doubt.
I'm here, you say
and hands out, poised to fall or fly
this may be just enough
to get us there.

Godson

There he lies, tender as chicken,
trussed up in soft cotton,
burping portentously like an old man.

In his wobbling skull there is a thread-thin crack,
and his swollen stomach and round fists
are covered with tissue-light, ribbon-smooth skin,
as if he were about to break into blossom.

Instead, he farts, smiles, and issues his verdict,
impressive even without his judge's wig.
His lips, burnished with invisible kisses
form the roundest 'o' of a gull's cry.

He stares with perfect equanimity
at the world of this room around him.
He seems unperturbed by his own fragility,
and merely frowns and raises a chubby hand.

We inspect each other calmly,
and when I pass a finger along his cheek,
he reaches up to grab my hair.
Still solemn, he burps, nods once, then closes his eyes,
as if to indicate
I will do.

Visit to the Former Museum of American Atrocities: Saigon, Vietnam

Aerial views: the country laid out like a tablecloth
in primary colours before chemical warfare, pastels after.
The babies in jars: babies with two heads, four arms.
Babies with seams in their skin,
the ragged stitches too weak to keep them together.

Then the photographs;
soldiers holding a head by its hair,
the tatters of the neck hanging limp like drying dough.
They bare their teeth like dogs that have learned to smile,
point – *look ma, no hands!*
They squat with ghosts of grins next to strings of ears,
brown mushrooms dried in the hard sun.

Outside we meet a monk with an Asian face and an American smile.
He sells watercolours in his temple,
laughs while he counts dollars, wearing
sneakers white as capped teeth under his brown hooded robe.

Down in the town we rent bikes with no brakes.
Wheels and legs tear along from all directions
towards a cataclysmic crash which never comes.
Families of four balance on a single bike,
a domestic circus trick.

It takes a while for it to sink in.
The trick is to keep your eyes straight ahead.
When you work up enough speed,
take your feet off the pedals and soar through.
Trust in the air itself to carry you.

Remember (To One Who Sleeps)

If the curtains part to show
another curtain, covering a light
which falls in shadows on my face;
making my breath float,
my voice tender,
my arms ringed with bright kept promises

Remember, it is you behind the curtain,
your voice low and echoing my own.
Remember, the curtain parts and closes at our asking.
(You stir in sleep, sweat lightly on my breast,
sing through a slumberous limb.)

It is nothing to speak in darkness
where you see what you wish to,
where invisibility aids imagination.

Here in the afternoon, both bright and dark
behind our curtains, we are truer to ourselves
and the light outside, the light inside.

We see all this in light unobscured, by curtains parted
by willing hands. If we trust each other
enough to leave each other, and then return,
we will always have this corner of this afternoon, this sun
to call our own.

Skin

They shed pieces of themselves each day,
like insects shucking skin, their particles fall,
the flecks sifting and shifting in dust.

Each week she sweeps them up from the floor,
aware of the fragments she cannot catch,
the skin that worms its way to the couch's core.

She knows as she sits that the cushions hold
the traces of their old selves, their young skin,
just as her body remembers the one inside it.

Back then even sweeping was fun,
interrupted by his fingers coursing electric,
her skin taut and sure beneath them.

Now, when she sees the impressions
they have left at each end of the couch,
she beats them out with a vigorous hand.

She sees the particles of dust and skin
fly up in a cloud of old self and new self,
imagines that they introduce themselves in mid air.

Mute on Light

I have a fear of ordinary words,
the way they conspire to make fun
of your extraordinary intention.

Egg, tea, wash, comb,
tangle the clean lines of ideals, hope, love.

Wiping the tabletop, watching
the sun lick the gleam of water away,
I wonder where the new words are.

The language that would describe
the explosions of light which accompany
the hours I spend with shop, meal, sleep.

I feel the small grey cells itch
and scratch out their longing,

just under the hair I brushed this morning
as I watched the rivers of shadow form
in a bed of disordered and vulnerable linen.

Dust hangs in the air, suspended by
a mysterious waiting.

It isn't waiting for pan, brush, sack.
If I could hear,
it might be lilting the words that the light whispers
as it pushes the frames of windows wider
or eats objects alive until they disappear into blindness.

Fishing

Sam was a galunky kind of guy,
my cousin says. *He walked like this.*
He takes on a bow-legged swagger
that makes us laugh. *And boy,*
could he drink beer. He lifts his hand,
tipping imaginary cans in quick succession.
He talked real fast too. Back then we laughed,
asked what was the rush? Never slowed him any.
Girls loved him. He was such a big guy,
think they figured he must have a big heart.

My cousin slows a little in his walk,
tugs on his ear to remember more.

We hung out a lot and unless he was excited,
talking fast, he was real quiet, would just sit,
stare out to space like he was someplace else.
Maybe he was thinking about the girl he loved
who died one winter, fell through the ice
as she was skating towards him.
She was only twenty feet away, her arms out wide.
They say he was there all night,
smashed the ice in a hundred places to find her.
They pulled her out in the Spring.
I think when he talked so fast
he was trying to forget,
like the words would fill up the space she left.

My cousin stops in the road,
brushes imaginary hair from his eyes.

I lost touch for some time, years went by.
I didn't hear from Sam, neither of us
were much use at letter writing.
Then one summer I came home to visit,

bumped right into him in a store downtown.
He talked real slow, like he was a clock
that had wound down. He said he'd taken up fishing.
He said he didn't much care for fish
but when he flung the line out hard,
heard the whir as it spun out over the water,
saw the river winking and glinting at him,
he felt he could catch anything.

Movement in Jazz

Tiny pubic hairs litter the bed; hieroglyphs,
little question marks,
poignant scraps of dead life.

I am a scavenger, I lean into the sheets
to catch the scent of what is already past and faint.

You are singing a scat in the shower.
I strain for the glimpses of your voice
in the hiss and muffle of water.

I strive for sense in your notes
through the same crackling distance of a foreign radio station.

You have been teaching me jazz life,
its relaxed wordlessness,
the threads of ingenuity in the tides of its long wails.

Under the sheets, I listen to a string quartet,
the adagio sticky and sweet on my tongue.

You come back from the shower,
still damp. I lean over to lick your shoulder,
taste the citric tang.
The jazz plays in the background,
circling and questioning, a little sour.

Later, as I make the bed,
I brush the question marks from the sheets,
stretching the cover firm over the mattress,
covering up any gaps.

The Voice

(For Anita Cerquetti, soprano, retired 1961)

You were discovered at a wedding,
bride to the rafters,
where your voice, diffusing,
soothed the splinters of the cantankerous wood.
A man said:
'You have a treasure in your throat,'
tears still standing out astonished in his eyes.

You had lungs of liquid silver.
Your tongue slowly drew each note's outline,
then stained it with colour,
or left it black and white to whisper plainly.
Your palate round, fine, full,
the voice rising like gold vapour,
condensing to an alchemist's dream.

Your arias, safe from the age of irony,
conduct a heart's passage, distil joy.
Your voice a reminder of trees at twilight,
folding melancholy between their darkening branches.
You are aching after what we had and have no longer;
our faith in the conquest of beauty, now
even beauty is open to suspicion.

Touching Nothing

Lying flat out on the grass late at night
outshivering the cold and letting the damp
become your first skin

You suddenly see the sky,
feel it descend in one heady blinding rush.

You are shrunk
to a scalp on a narrow pole,
dried-out, dry-mouthed
and tortured by territory.

The moon reflects your own eye,
peering with no pupil, a great mass
of unblinking white.

Then, just as the weight becomes oppressive,
just before you roll over and turn your back
on the earth, you feel the pull of the rope.

Bound down and set free, in the mid-air skip
of a game of jump rope, you are between two worlds.

Understanding both in a language you cannot hear
or speak, you are deafened by an airy roar
and the plaintive, nebulous wail
of a radio that won't tune in.

Winning

Sometimes, when we make love, you bite your lip,
concentrating on our bodies, a melt of muscles.
You are taken up with nothing but flesh,
the flush of damp skin, my shakes of gasps.

It is a coup, a rush of arm and leg and mouth army,
pushing to claim new territory, to hear the opposition
beg for mercy.

In a way we are fighting, sometimes on the same side,
sometimes against each other.
This is why, afterwards, lying panting and exhausted
after a peak of effort,
our hearts thrusting up against our chests,
I am surprised to remember
your open-mouthed cry of surrender,
your collapse against me,
the words *I love you*.

Reversal

Rivers never reverse, he said as they walked towards town.
All the capillaries swelling with desire to get to the heart of the sea. She coughed.
Wait, she said, *something's caught my foot.* He quickly turned to help.
She took his arm gingerly as she untangled her shoe
from a condom's swollen finger.
As their glances snapped back up, only the corner of her eye flickered
but it was enough to see his pale face flame.
Nature's leftovers, and she laughed. Then stopped when he looked shocked.

It was at least half an hour to the old town's walls.
The river's sluggish today. Making conversation.
He was silent, walking ahead, his back stiff and affronted,
held up with hurt.
She sighed and watched the crisp bags sail like misshapen boats.
Wrappers breathed in air and lifted to drift in their company.

I thought this would be romantic. His voice falling flat on itself,
his shoulders hunched, his bravado ditched and bewildered.
She watched his six feet shrink to six years old.
A slide popped up in front of her,
a picture of them wandering along a meandering creek,
listening to it singing over the stones.
They were stepping over wild flowers
as gently as if they were spun glass.

She touched his arm, felt the soft cotton of his shirt.
Actually, it was quite a nice arm.
But it is romantic.
Uncertain, he waited for her to laugh. The river gurgled by them.
Ignoring the bubbles of scum that clung to the moss
they kissed to the sound of water.

On Dying I Realise the Significance of Religious Belief

You do not get last rites on the operating table,
it would not look optimistic.
So there was no chance for the last minute insurance
no opportunity to say 'I do' to the comforting clatter of long beads.

The doctors glided around me, hardly noticing
the body on which they were about to perform.
Dressed in their white coats and masks and gloves
they were as arrogant and graceful as swans.

Always a late developer, my pulse became a percussionist.
Perhaps now they'll take note, I thought.
But they were arguing about golf and I slipped away
as softly and smoothly as the elision when 'I am' becomes 'I'm not'.

Death was an ugly surprise.
I walked through a white gate labelled Arrivals
to be confronted with placards held by patient hands.
'Catholics' 'Protestants' 'Quakers' 'Muslims'
It was like arriving without the keys to your front door.

I searched for something, anything, in which I had once believed.
If only I had been a Buddhist at college like everyone else.
There they trotted, smiling and content, at peace.
I asked someone on their way to 'Baptists' where the Atheists were.

'Oh they fly into terminal B, you know, *second* class,'
he smiled smugly, sharing the joke, then pattered off to his new home.
The coaches were leaving, some of the newcomers
singing hymns in the back.

'Hello, you seem to be lost,' I turned, dazzled by the bells of the voice.
The flight attendant shimmered before me in translucent blue.
'Do you not have a destination?' it asked. I shook my head.
'This way please,' and it led me to a flight of stairs.

We climbed for what seemed like days, my legs like putty
when we reached the top. 'You'll be waiting here,' it said
gesturing to chairs which overlooked the runway.
From here you could see the planes arrive and the coaches leave.

'You did not choose,' the voice said, tinkling sadly
like Tinkerbell dying. 'I didn't choose,' I echoed
like a ghost in the dark. I sat and looked at my prospect.
Comings and goings. The other seats stretched on either side of me,
a desert of tired plastic.
'Always have a hobby for a rainy day,' my father said.
'You never know where you might get stuck.'

After an Argument We Didn't Have

All night, restless, I felt the inch of air between us,
the way we didn't fit skin to skin
or cleave our bones.
You slept; you are talented this way.
I stoked my anger, feeding it reason on reason,
smouldering in silence, hearing you breathe.
But as light came, sneaking in layers of brightness,
dissipating the dark and my blindness,
I noted how your shoulder blade pierced the air and the shadows,
and how you shifted, slightly, towards me.
My hand decided to trace the planes of the blade
unbidden, and as it felt the curve, remembered others.
The unsaid words which had bubbled on my tongue for hours
burst like flowers. My body pressed hard against you,
in beautiful betrayal, your warmth suffusing me
like amnesia. Next time, I promised,
nothing would wait until morning.

The Untouchables

Everything about them is smooth,
from the shaved planes and curves of their legs and cheeks
to their creamy milk walk, their liquidity
as their spines melt to sitting position.
The men, snug as gloves in their jackets and sunglasses,
the women, muscle-toned but soft-breasted, legs long and slim, lips sharp.

Their bags, nestling at their feet like lapdogs, spell out money,
and there is a lazy whisper of fine fabrics.
Their glance slides right through you.
You are conscious of your puckered shirt,
your stockings wrinkled like rolls of fat round your ankles.
Somehow you know these people never sweat.

Don't they leak blood, lose lovers, misplace important documents,
burn their fingers, knock their elbows,
yell too loudly at the kids just like everyone else?
The imagination slides off all attempts
to speculate what goes on behind their shaded, layered eyes.
There is not one word, one hair, one cell out of place.

You walk too fast, head down, past their seats,
the chrome café tables flash smugly like family silver.
You get back to your street: the thick broken slabs of pavement,
the urine-smelling, pockmarked trees.

Your kids tumble out the flaking front doors
a clump of clammy, grabby hands:
'Look what we .... look what I .... come and see.'
Their scabby knees, their knotted hair, their shirts bearing medals of food.
They are looking at you with huge toothy grins.
You are smiling back so hard you have to blink away tears.
There is nothing, absolutely nothing, perfect about them.

Fish

Slow as batter, the river runs heavy-bellied beside us.
We're in the roundest part of summer.

At first we see nothing, just the dark mass of water,
plaited weeds weaving over stones.

Then we catch a glint of fish, like the wink
of sun in the water's mud green surface.

They are dark spectres, would be slick as oil
to the touch, if we were allowed to touch.

Well armoured, scales flashing notes of silver,
they play hide and seek on a chord of stones.

They tease us, bending cat-like round corners,
but their surprised blinkless eyes miss nothing.

We wait, watch this cold-blooded, distant dance,
held in the shadow of our former life.

Stitches

I stand in front of the mirror and cry over my body
the way a mother cries over a dead child,
feeling nothing can change this grief for the lost flesh,
this hatred for the cold dead chance of life.

The doctor said, learn to love this line, in it you can read
the words of the stitches that saved you.
But they are mute in the presence
of the full round promise that neighbours them.

There remains just one target for the mouth of a child,
one target for the hands and lips of a man.

I think of going back to the hard white bed,
offering up my other breast like a virgin sacrifice.
Perhaps with two thin white lines, a symmetry of knives,
I could return to the chaste simplicity
of the young girl's vest,
her flat chest clean and brave,
carving out her long lean line
before the heaviness of blood and flesh anchors her,
mooring her like a slip of a boat
tied to the edge of the sea.
But the thought of giving up the swell I can hold in my hand
brings me to the mirror and the mind of the mother:
once you've had, you cannot unhave.
The rhythm of the flesh once started cannot be hushed,
it throbs unending, collecting together the secrets of cells.

Here, I can feel it under the cool crest of the scar,
it is there.
It remembers its work and its love.
As it mourns itself in the delicate lace
of its tight white lines,
it tells me I am alive.

Horses

We ride like horses
Me on top like a rocking horse
or you on top galloping
into breathlessness
When I rock we laugh
and lick the gathering wet heat
and arch our backs and kick
Slowly the ground disappears
beneath us and the need to soar
swoops up all laughter into intent
When you strain for the last lengths
we leave the country at last
and head out to the ocean
Nuzzling your shoulder, your shining coat
I find myself close to tears
so certain am I that it could
be our last ride
that you are the winning horse
and that we might never find our way home.

The Herd

They lift their heads, mildly curious,
necks moving soberly slow,
then bend back to grass.

They lumber from one patch to the next,
a clumsy grace in their hind-swaying gait.

Their joints are well-oiled, their flanks fat,
but they stare as you pass like glass-gazed victims,
imprisoned in the outside air.

The wise wet eyes are almost haunting,
almost daunting.
They remind you that only the farmer gave you permission
to cross this land.

The horse-heavy breathing
makes you walk a little faster.

A trespasser, your boots brush the grass with embarrassment,
the awkwardness of one who's not at home.

You reach the gate, the object of perspective.
From the other side they return to what they were,
just cows.

They stare back at you, ambiguous.
You remember a childhood picturebook:
'What do cows give?' 'Milk.'
'What do cows say?' 'Moo.'

As if animals were drawn by human hand,
stay within their outline's bounds.

Drawing

I am a child's drawing, a mouth on a stick,
a drone twisting up towards him like smoke.
He listens to me, his head cocked
to one side, little ears all over his face.

I go home to my other half, my other stick.
We scream in tight-throated whispers
so as not to disturb the children,
who are hanging like monkeys over the bannisters,
their arms clinging and clinging to the hard wood.

Late at night I get up and wander through the house.
My other stick's mouth is slight and delicate,
one hand clenched, one arm drawn over
to my side of the bed.

I showed him the drawing my daughter made:
Mummy, daddy, sister, and mummy's friend.
He said, *Look how it's all in black and white,
don't kids usually like to draw in colour?*

In the kitchen, everything grey in the dark,
I think of his ear against a pillow,
quiet without
my mouth, my voice, my eager
clamourous hands.

They learn scale later, says her teacher,
smiling as he points at the house, small in the foreground
with the stick figures towering behind.
I am especially big, growing out of the house.
A giant above my children
but with arms long enough to reach their hands.
No, I say, *I think she got everything right.*

Lying in Bed

We talk of how I do not love you enough,
the conversation is like one long nail
down a wide-eyed blackboard.

And I have to lie quietly there, breathing
small breaths like in hide and seek
so you cannot guess how close you are.

How can I tell you that you turned down my heart
like a volume switch, waiting as it was to hear
the words that are tumbling too late from your mouth.

How can I tell you that it isn't my fault that emotions
eroded on a daily, infinitesimal basis, as slow
and inevitable as feet over marble steps.

So I tell you lies: I tell you that maybe with time
I tell you that yes, we have had so much together
I tell you there is something to work on

I tell you I love you and lie there holding my breath
waiting for the sirens to sear the air.

Eggshells

You sit, belly-full,
unconscious of your queenliness.
You trace your stretch marks,
sketching answers with your finger-tips
for the fat-handed child who clutches
your vulnerable knee.

You see no joy in such heaviness.
You watch your old life swing by on disdainful hips,
and mourn coke-can rings worn on slight fingers,
fast-food jewellery to throw away.

Out of sight, you'd be surprised to see the eyes slide
back to you and beyond. You are potent,
placed in a parallel life.

They laugh and shake out their thin limbs.
They are tauntingly light, ready to float
if and when they should wish to.
You are moored in a blank bay
where your only visitors are bored tourists.

Even the day seems obese, obscene in the way flowers
suck all freshness from the air,
replacing it with perfume, thickly sweet.

But now the fat-handed child brings you a present,
an ant. Alive in a tight fleshy fist,
it remains still for one vital moment, quivering.

Then it turns and runs down the child's arm to the floor,
picking up a piece of eggshell twice its size.

The eggshell has turned translucent in the sun,
lit within like stained glass. The ant carries it away,
sure of itself, taking its time, translating in its circular route
the lines on your skin.

Water

The moment after she told him
she no longer loved him *that* way,
his face flowered into water.
The tears ran upward and sideways
and down. She found herself wondering
how he could cry in all directions.

And as she wondered she realized
that the salt on her lips came from him,
that this was the first salt she had drawn,
the first blood. The shadows cleared from his face,
the shadows that had clouded out the love
she had tried again and again to give him.

And now his face hung over hers,
his skin glimmering silver and salt.
And she gazed gravely back at him,
her hand rising to touch, her eyes watching
the tears running up, and sideways, and down,
defying gravity, defying.

She thinks, she thought then,
watching the star rays of his tears,
his eyes watering the compressed dry earth of her heart,
how grass will find a crack in concrete, and grow.

The Surgeon's Wife

He presses her into silence; folds her into the dough of it,
where it fills her ears and mouth as tightly as a cork.
She watches as his butcher's hands, cased in too much flesh,
part the sticky kiss of salami slices, tenderly.
He cuts bread so thick it falls like lead.

He tells her where he is going, a litany of domesticity
to which she must religiously assent:
to the post office to post a letter, to the shop to buy food,
to the hospital to save patients.
He proves his existence, and there is nothing over.

Immersing herself in the bath, watching the water
carefully enclose each knee, she pictures his veins.
They would be narrow, narrower
than the glistening thread of a snail
before it's snapped and turned by a spade in earth.

Her thighs – which she thinks look like legs of lamb – the butcher!
tip up in the water, straining towards air.
She forgets for a moment the weight of the objects around her,
the weight of her flesh. He has fattened his stock.
Her solidity asserts his own. She is the pie under his fingers.

Words swarm in her blood like bees in spring.
During his cutting hours, she leaks hope.
But on his return, she feels her life leaning away,
and his – silent, precise – towards her.
Each stake of the white picket fence slices its way,
securing her future.

How A Vegetable Can Change Your Life (Momentarily)

This morning you woke up and wondered
if it was worth the effort
to repeat the same day.

Now you're standing in the kitchen, hands at your sides,
having forgotten what you were about to do.

The pregnant clouds drowse outside,
unconscious of this miniature agony.
You wish it would rain.

It comes without warning, this non-feeling,
this numbness. You ask it questions
but it stares at you like the unmade bed;
not ready to get into, not easy to get out of.

You are overwhelmed by this need
for a reason to breathe. You panic.
You are alone in the kitchen.
Then you breathe out, a long sigh.

In the middle of the table sits a pumpkin.
Superbly fat, it spreads its orange stomachs outward
like a tumoured flower. It has the beery smile
of a belly that props up bars.

It exudes the motherly smell of cinnamon,
the memory of someone who will hold your hand.

You imagine a vase full of vegetables,
vibrant and firm, sure of themselves in their rough skins.
They say – as they give off a plain, earthy smell –
Touch what you love, work with your hands.

Slipping

It's the pauses, not the words.
The way your glance slides to the other side,
away from me.
You cough more often, clear your tense throat,
but there's nothing there.
Nothing there that you would allow yourself to say.
I watch the veins in your neck, the steady slow pulse.

Once these pauses were honey, sliding between
rushes, an onslaught of thoughts we knew were shared.
We had confidence then, convinced the light would hold.

The lights dim, slipping on a scale, making them tip
towards ground. A car dreams past, our heads tilt
to it, to the window, to an outside distraction,
escape.

You frown, as if concentrating. We both know
this is a pretence to hide blankness.
The intangible feelings have condensed to a tiny drop.
Not oil, not an essence of richness as we first thought.
But fluid that evaporates even in cooling temperatures.

This is the trouble. That the things unseen float
between visibility and invisibility.
Reaching out to grasp them will only increase their tendency
to slip away. We watch air, wait till the last tendrils
twist out of sight, carried by water.
Facing each other, we find we are watching walls.

Pasta

In the yellow kitchen her pink hands
play with creamy dough. Squares of sun frame
things that shine; spoons, cups, hair.

She sits the fat belly on the table.
She pokes it with one finger, it dimples.

Stroked with flour, her rolling pin
works roundness to flatness,
teases out a thin cream sheet.

She picks up the sheet with a nimble pinch,
feeds it into the teeth of the steel machine.

She turns the handle, smiling at me
though I know she is tired, not very happy.
She hangs the frail strips on chairs, on doors.

As the dampness lifts they start to flutter.
She hangs them lightly over her arm, padding to the stove.

She boils water, opens wine, puts vegetable in pots.
Lights click. Smells blossom.
Everything feels suddenly invited.

Steps

You go click clack click clack across the floor,
give nothing away but the soles of your shoes.

But, attuned to the weight of your foot,
I hear the spleen in the sharp rap of your heel,

feel your ache to crush the floor with your toes.
I consider – 'What's wrong?' will get 'Nothing.'

So sit while we stay on the same footing.
I know the steps and silence of this dance.

My own right foot begins, gently, to twitch.
You stride from door to drawer, six steps reduced

to four by energetic rage. You jerk
drawers open as if they're hiding something,

rattle knives with a frustrated longing.
It's not the chicken's blood you'd like to spill.

As the preparations come to an end,
I hear submission in your lightened tread,

as if weary of the war path we know
so well, too well. I needn't even look

to see you turn, to hear your toe stirring
the floor with thought. I could make it easy,

take the first step, offer apologies,
but I prefer to measure your mind's change,

watch you count (for next time's sake) how many
steps it takes before I come to meet you.

Reading a Biology Book: Chapter One, Characteristics of Life

1. MOVEMENT
Living things move of their own accord

Unless pushed. This happens.
We go to work, to jobs that are dull. We fall in love,
against our will. There are extremes.
People get pushed by unseen hands,
deliverance to the next stage.
I would like you to be delivered to me in a neatly wrapped package.
It would be nice if it was of your own accord,
if you climbed into the box yourself,
a flower clenched between your teeth.

2. SENSITIVITY
Living things are sensitive to their environment

Sensitivity is a malady. Once it was a virtue, of sorts.
Snivelling does not inspire love. If you want steps forward,
take several back. This is the law of desire.
Tears are often the precipitation of anger. You do not understand this,
or the shades of our environment.
Late at night, I hear the ghost of our house, water running
in a parallel room, a parallel life.
Sometimes, we would both like to be next door.

3. FEEDING
Living things feed

Some eat more than others, and tastes vary.
Your silence and your insistence on keeping your limbs to yourself
create a nagging scratch in my stomach, a low-key sense of starvation.
You push the plate away when I offer a heaped helping,
making up for all the empty plates in the world.
You are polite, you say, 'Thank you.'

4. RESPIRATION
Living things respire

Some people (see how easy it is to apportion blame)
take up more than their share. Or perhaps I don't know how to breathe.
No-one taught me to cup the air in my mouth, curl it up in the tongue,
feel it fill the lungs, imagining their pink dampness,
their walls pushing out gratefully, suspending panic
and suffocation.
On mountains the air is thin. I sit perched on one,
wobbling on the pinnacle and wondering
who will teach me how to fly.

5. EXCRETION
Excretion is the removal from the body
of waste products which result from normal life processes

I watch you pick meat from a bone with your tusk white teeth.
It may be my bone. Recently I have lost the strength in my spine,
due to life processes which I cannot call 'normal'.
I am living proof of the Victorian belief that women need corsets
to keep them upright. I waver between the hours,
clutching the backs of chairs,
moulding myself to sofas, watching you pick at the debris of meals.

6. REPRODUCTION
Unless reproduction occurs populations of organisms will diminish and eventually
disappear as their members die from old age, disease, accidents,
attacks from other organisms

Which brings into question what or who you are, in that order.
My blood questions your species,
my blood slows when I hear certain tones in your voice,
a detachment which freezes the passage to my heart,
an organ which can no longer translate any message.
You give birth to our children in your head,
like the god you may think you are.

You describe the pain and the difficulty.
I look on in horror,
reproducing the same doubts over and over.

7. GROWTH
Most animals grow until they reach maturity

Note: some never do.
I look over to a mirror-backed chest, full of glasses
that reflect themselves and the light. I reflect myself in the glass,
seeing through to the backs of things,
which however many times repeated,
remain the backs, and impenetrable.
We shed skin in bed, rubbing our lives against each other,
leaving old layers behind.
We wait for the thing we've grown to take root,
or to one day turn round and find
it has died in its dark red pot.

Learning the Language

You told me story on story of your past, rewriting history
till the air was thick and impenetrable before us.
We saw each other through the fog of our hopes.
I was a cut-out daughter then,
blurred around the edges, pudding faced and brained.

Then I was thrown into the shape of my life,
hurtling through space until I broke through the orbit
that had circled us since I was a child.
Time sharpened me, cutting my features
clear and keen as a sculptor's knife.

You travelled, learned languages pedantically, insisting
your projected self should be an educated man,
refusing to sound any less than you are.
I began to see that there were cracks in your lunar surface.

And now, I visit you in the country where you live.
Things have moved on.
You are secure again in the meanings of words.
We sit, all grown up, drinking coffee.
We watch a woman as she pushes out her feet in a slow dance.
You translate for me – she is complaining about the fit of her shoes.
You say, Before you understand a language,
you think that the words that surround you
are heavier than they are, that they hold the answers to the world.
You are disappointed. I nod.

You are no longer like a planet through a telescope,
whole, incandescent. We are joined.
We are the pieces of broken sun reflected in water,
knocking against each other, edges fitting where they touch,
luminous, imperfect.

Things

The non-arrival of the things you ordered
pile up in the hall.

The things you wished for don't appear either,
in every corner, every spare space.

You pick your way through them, carefully,
to call and complain.

A woman at the end of a cold wire says
'The manager will tell you the same,
tomorrow, they will come tomorrow.'

You slam the phone down
and the cord gets caught round your wrist.

The invisible things pile up and spill over,
seep under doors and through windows.

You pride yourself on your skill
at keeping container-tight.

You find lists of the things you want, the things you need.
You laugh and shake your head.
That night you dream of empty rooms.

The dreams escalate as the possessions invade,
you dream of fields and peopleless places.

Making dinner, surrounded by ingredients and spices,
you fantasize about ripping apart a Japanese house,
watching the paper blow to the wind.

You think of the three pigs, making friends with the wolf,
setting fire to straw.

Pretence

You had nightmares and turned, tucked up, to your side,
embryonic and convulsing.
The helplessness of watching someone dream
struck me, my hands prayed over your skin.

You turned from me, as far as the yard of bed allowed,
chasing me away with the chill of your absence.
I reached to you with my fingertips: shakily, once.

I could hear the train you were catching the next day,
a phantom, thrumming with impatience,
the doors slamming on the hours.

My desire to section out your skin with my hands and mouth,
to listen to your heart strike out the minutes of the night,
collapsed like an exhausted bird trying to escape glass.

Perhaps the next morning was worse,
with your busy cheerfulness abrasive
and me feeling foolish, and chastened
and suddenly uncertain if this city was all you were leaving.

I clutched calm as if it was driftwood
smiling at you like arms stretched out.
You kissed me goodbye, a fleeting wing on my lips
and I turned and walked jauntily down the steps
as if my whole life was round the corner.

Caterpillar

Although the pupa outwardly looks inert and resting, inside it is a bubbling cauldron of activity as the caterpillar is literally liquefied, then reassembled…. into a very different creature. It's still not fully understood how this process occurs

Science slides away from me; algebra rearranges my thoughts
into question marks knocking their heads against walls.

But this strikes me, these lines on mysterious biology,
on a life form transforming itself like alchemy.

From slow sloth to powdery flight, and in between liquid fire.
Transmutation. A witch's brew.

      ***

There is this in the caterpillar's life I like:
the second chance for beauty,
the life of toil rewarded,
the sumptuous display after hugging walls,
a shy dancer caught up by the music,
a Cinderella figure whirling in shining shoes.

      ***

The puzzles of insect life belong to us too.
Have you noticed that when they tell you where our organs are
they don't tell you how they move.
How the stomach shrinks and stretches like an accordion,
or spins in confined abandon like the spokes on a wheel.
Or how the lungs tighten,
the veins ache.

How the heart, from firmness, dissolves,
reforming into something that can fly.

Soon We Will Meet

Soon we will meet and shake hands
and talk of politics or sport or even the weather
of anything except of how my mouth once knew the lines of your body
and how you'd smile under my fingers until you fell into breathing.

And you will ask polite questions about what I am doing
and close the door on how you used to know
what my day would be and how it would be
and the way you would fit into it somewhere.

And we will remember mutual friends
but not how you used to stroke my neck
or how you cupped my back with your hands
until I arched and relaxed into the bones of your body.

And we will laugh at a joke and startle ourselves at the closeness it brings
and pause and fall into an awkward silence.

And then I will ask after your new girlfriend and then wish I hadn't
and you will ask after my new boyfriend and then wish you hadn't
and then we will finish the rest of our drinks too fast
and say we really must be going
but how we must keep in touch.

And then we will hug briefly and awkwardly
and feel each others' fingers burn into our backs
and you will walk away and I will walk away
and something very small will break inside.

Nature's Braille

From here I can see the daisies,
their yolk faces addled with grins.
One has refused to open
even in this irate heat.
The grass pricks my bare skin,
cross with my weight.
When I rise it leaves an indent
of crosses and lines.
You call it Nature's braille,
reach out your hand to read me.
I roll away, frown at the irascible sun.

The Absence of Lungs

I imagine your lungs in the gap between the sheets
exhaling air to push the skin of your belly
up close against my back, our minuscule hairs
mixing and twining like blades of grass.

I imagine us breathing in tandem,
following the undulations of near sleep.
Your lungs fill for the sheer joy of breath
and the touch of the small of my back.

I see the pinkness of them, giving and distributing,
the rest of your body grateful and red with life.
I wonder whether, the next morning,
I will wake first and watch you sleeping.

The absence of your lungs adds to the others;
the absence of your legs, buttocks, back, arms, face.
The fact that I haven't even met you yet
doesn't detract from this dabbing pain.

From an aerial view, our shapes are negligible and separate,
pieces of leftover skin and blood and cells and bone,
something that was whole and moved on.
This awareness does not bring peace,

just a shrinkage of body parts.
So, in between now and the time when I may meet you
I practice breathing for survival, filling my lungs
to the utmost, making them strong.

I imagine that you are practising too
and this stops the dispirited bubbles forming in my blood,
gives me the ability to breathe with a full set of lungs
on one tank of air.

Thinking Ahead

Last week, I bought you a duck, all wood
with a string to pull it and make it quack.
You'll like it. We'll fight over who has the next go.

I have to hold back from the tiny dresses and the miniature rompers,
after all, I don't know what you are yet.

Sometimes, I can almost feel you knitting yourself inside me,
sorting the genes like building blocks, picking out the best of me.
I like to think this is how it would work.

I miss you. I miss your hand in mine, its tiny palm,
the fingers so dimpled I feel like I'm holding a smile.

I sit here thinking of you and all the fun we'll have.
Hurry up now, can't you see all the twinkles in my eye?

Sooner than Now

I would like to be watched by you
as I move softly about the room,
putting traces of our day
carefully away in drawers,
shutting us gently into night
and into sheets hugging
the outlines of our arms wrapped round
each other.

Sooner than now I would have you speaking
your night voice, velvety, low,
folding me to you,
as we prepare to turn out the last light,
turning in the rising dark
to begin another chapter
of this book,
each leaf of which I can hardly wait
to turn.

Sooner than now I would be laughing with you,
forgetting the original wit and falling into the
pure joy of like meets like, like loves like,
while we are surrounded by gardens
planted by loving hands,
growing steadily, scenting air,
as if each path and flowerbed
was our own.

Sooner than now I would place the final fear
behind me, accept you as the gift
that is always
the very thing I wished for,
unwrap you with sure but tender hands,
keeping you close, happy,
ever, sooner, now.

Doing it Ourselves

(For Neil)

They didn't tell me that the purchase of a home
brings with it a whole new lexicon to learn.
The language springs out of the boxes we open,
the words fall casually from the lips of men who like to straddle things,
exhaling strange and exotic terms like smoke.

Lath-and-plaster, epoxy-resin, spoke shaves, soffit, and grout.
Noggings, ratchet, lead flashings, verge drips, screed.
The words leak from every room and exterior wall
and I have no idea what they mean.
But when I look them up in our DIY handbook
I am constantly disappointed.

Surely 'closure' bricks I should have thrown
at my ex-boyfriends,
and sarking follows a hammer on your thumb.
A spring-toggle fixing fastens a child's coat,
flue liner is protection for a winter cold.
A stud partition is a gigolo's girlfriend,
a shallow-seal trap will be banned any day,
spiral balances are a dancer's feet.

And a float finish is what we come to after a hard day
of painting, and cleaning, and nodding as the straddling men
suck their teeth and shake their multiple heads.

It is what we move towards after we have opened two bottles of wine
and drunk them and climbed laughing into the bath
on the bare concrete floor.

It is where we lie happy and aching after we have made love
on our mattress and talked about the time when we can afford a bed.

It is the dance-light feeling after we have arranged our limbs
to fit as close as the tongue and groove panelling in the hall,

reflecting that this is the it
we can do very nicely ourselves.

We, Who Cannot Sleep

(For my husband)

We, who cannot sleep, who talk ourselves
past wakefulness, then, past exhaustion,
slept that night.
Your bed big enough
for a luxurious cat-stretch,
yet the two of us
wound round each other like softened twine.

In the hooded half-light of the heavy-curtained
room, round and full with our night's breath,
I woke to find you watching me.
And I, who don't like to be looked at too long,
looked back,
pressed my face to yours,
felt it natural and right to see you
watching over me.

The First Trimester

Turns every soft-focused notion of motherhood on its stomach.
My body is thrown into an orbit of non-stop
physical sensations and symptoms, none of which
are appropriate to bring up at a dinner party.

It is not a time of serenity but a time of testiness
not a time of gentleness but of sudden sickness,
bone-softening, skin-itching exhaustion.
Green-tinged days pass so slowly as to make the prospect
of nine months suddenly seem longer
than the moment when you realise
you might turn out to be even more like your parents
than they are.

Reading about you, and what you are doing to me,
does not help matters.
I am a host organ, carrying an alien
who threatens to bear an uncanny resemblance
to those members of the family
we most dislike.

I feel sure that you will inherit my ears and his feet,
the genes of our stubbornness combined will surely
produce a mule of such intractability
that you will refuse to be potty-trained
forever.

I do not glow, I do not move with new-found grace,
I am not more acceptant of the world at large.
Instead, I wonder how it has taken me so long to notice
that there is not a shred of sanity in our surroundings,
that even my husband, the solution till now to all fretting,
is unable to solve the problem of getting you out with no pain
a problem to which I am devoting
many hours of thought.

I think I may reach that mirage of serene sweetness
in about four or five years time,
when you are young enough to indoctrinate
and too young yet to hate us.
Until then, or until the promised land of the second 'tri'
(as the initiated can say),
I distract myself with the books I can still read,
and the sleep I can still enjoy,
and try not to dwell on carrots.

Darling Fool Child

Now that you're nearly here, I watch the young ones,
worrying, wishing you were tighter within me.

The boys, all outsized hands and feet,
gangle over walls,
their faces smeared with disdainful leers
too old for their faces,
and not quite hiding
their bewildered bones.

The girls, all hanging hair and slit-eyed glances,
lean into each other,
away from the chilly front of cold shoulders
which can strip them
in an unpoised second
to their raw, unready selves.

And you, my darling fool child,
you thrust yourself against my belly, already
longing for this, wishing your first greedy gulp of air,
the taste and breadth of your first sky.
You don't realise that the days
bring you relentlessly closer
to the heartless present of youth.

My unknown sweetheart,
enjoy the bubble of your existence
and our mutual anticipation,
don't wish the stretched, plucked strings of love
with all their mute agony and lip-bitten joy
a day too soon.

Enjoy your making, your last moments
of understanding and control,
while my heart contracts with each kick

thinking of all the young years
you have yet to endure.

My strange love, I wish you a swift passage
to the safe, cosy apathy and regret
of your middle age.
My unborn babe,
be old before your time.